SHE

Ekla Cholo Re

A story meant to motivate all and sundry
irrespective of their circumstances!

Dr. Shayan Haq

Santosh Avvannavar

Edited by : Rajashree Ghosh

For information contact : info@hoffen.in

www.facebook.com/She.EklaCholoRe

First Edition: Oct 2015

Contents

Disclaimer

The author of this book recommend parental guidance or to follow the country Law for children to pick and/or read this book. Although an attempt has been made to bring the thoughts with sanity keeping most of the cultures in mind, yet it's challenging to completely deny or avoid some cultural understanding. The names and characters in the stories all are all fictitious and they do not represent any true persons, caste, creed, culture, religion and region. Even if any such corrélations are found in true nature, they're purely coincidental.

This book is dedicated to: -

The Almighty God,

Parents,

Amrita Foundation

&

Raghunath Babu Are (My Best Buddy)

Acknowledgement

We would like to thank the Almighty for giving us the ability to pen stories in his glory. We thank our parents for their unconditional love and support. We express our gratitude to our best friends, Sameer Mirji, Vasudha Mirji, and Amresha M for their presence during our times of trials. We also extend our gratitude to our mentors Meena R Chandawarkar, P V Ramana, N K Narasimhan, Suchita Khanna, Avinash Himanshu, Rahul Nair and Parul Thakur (motivators). We also thank Dr. Lokesh Patil (M.D.), Vineet Singh (Software Engineer at TCS), Saurav Kumar (MBA), and Nithish J, Abhilash Alwandi (Software Engineer), Raghavendra Kumar Reddy (Consultant) co-author of 'Get a Job WITHOUT an Interview', Subhashis Panda co-author of 'Be a B.A.', Prof. Shrihari (Faculty at NITK, Surathkal), Dr.Bhagyashree, Mr. Sharanbasavaraj Patil & Mr. Sanjeevkumar Yaliballi (Dept of Social Work, KSWU, Bijapur), Firdous Shabnam, Shilpa Patil, Pastor Anil and Sister Glory for their constant support.

We also extend our thanks to all the reviewers for reviewing 'Adhuri Prem Kahaniya', 'Dear Wife, Your

Husband is not a Superhero', 'Second Heart', 'Get a Job WITHOUT an Interview', 'Be a B.A', 'Surrogate Author', 'Title is Untitled', 'Black, Grey and White', 'God's Table', 'The Departing Point', and 'Umbilical Cord'.

We also thank Amrita Foundation for HRD (www.amritafoundation.wordpress.com) for allowing us to pen our thoughts since May 2012. We thank our editor Rajashree Ghosh for doing the necessary edits. We thank people involved in formatting the book and cover page design for their efforts in making this book elegant and beautiful. Last but not the least, we would like to thank all our dear students as well!

Introducing
'She'

'She in he, he in She' is something unusual, unacceptable and is seen as a 'different' behavioral trait in the society. We, the 'normal' beings 'pretend' that such people do not exist, albeit for our own convenience. For us, life is very simple as we only acknowledge two categories – male and female – and we mock and rebuke someone stuck in between. We hardly understand the pain of remaining trapped in someone else's body – a boy trapped in a woman's body and/or vice versa. Perhaps, we are mere puppets in the hands of our social conditioning and thus we 'reject' them and push them towards social ostracization. But, in spite of all odds, exceptional talents are born to show the world that hope still exists.

'She' is a story of one such brave heart who is set to explore an identity that is often untitled, that does not belong anywhere, definitely not under the 'he' or 'she' bracket because of the pre-conceived notion that each one possesses. Thus, the protagonist begins a long search for identity that is born out of a strong desire for getting a Title from being Untitled through poem, nature, some broken moments and the creator's call. The motivation to write 'She' came from the famous "Ekla Cholo Re", which is part of Rabindranath Tagore's song anthology Baul, published in Bhandar magazine in 1905. The song exhorts about the journey of 'She' to continue despite the fear of abandonment from others. The song goes like this, "Jodi Tor Dak Shune Keu Na Ase Tobe Ekla Cholo Re" meaning "If no one responds to your call, then go your own way alone".

যদি তোর ডাক শুনে কেউ না আসে তবে একলা চলো রে।

একলা চলো, একলা চলো, একলা চলো, একলা চলো রে॥

যদি কেউ কথা না কয়, ওরে ও অভাগা,

যদি সবাই থাকে মুখ ফিরায়ে সবাই করে ভয়—

তবে পরান খুলে

ও তুই মুখ ফুটে তোর মনের কথা একলা বলো রে॥

যদি সবাই ফিরে যায়, ওরে ওরে ও অভাগা,

যদি গহন পথে যাবার কালে কেউ ফিরে না চায়—

তবে পথের কাঁটা

ও তুই রক্তমাখা চরণতলে একলা দলো রে॥

যদি আলো না ধরে, ওরে ওরে ও অভাগা,

যদি ঝড়-বাদলে আঁধার রাতে দুয়ার দেয় ঘরে-

তবে বজ্রানলে

আপন বুকের পাঁজর জ্বালিয়ে নিয়ে একলা জ্বলো রে।।

Here is the translation in prose of the Bengali original rendered by Rabindranath Tagore himself.

If they answer not to your call walk alone
If they are afraid and cower mutely facing the wall,
O thou unlucky one,
open your mind and speak out alone.
If they turn away, and desert you when crossing the wilderness,
O thou unlucky one,
trample the thorns under thy tread,
and along the blood-lined track travel alone.
If they shut doors and do not hold up the light when the night is troubled with storm,
O thou unlucky one,
with the thunder flame of pain ignite your own heart,
and let it burn alone.

Year
1990

Good morning students! Today we will learn about '*AIDS, Homosexuality and We*'; let us begin with few cases. The first case is of Rubin, a twenty-five-year-old male. When he was in his teens, he along with his friend (a male) had stroked each other's orgasm in a sexual play. Although Rubin considers himself to be heterosexual, yet he masturbates thus showing signs of teenage sexual fantasy. While masturbating, he finds himself in an uneasy position because of his fantasies. Let's move on to our second case – that of Donald, who is in his mid-thirties, married and has a child. He has a healthy sexual life with his wife and is monogamous. However, once in every fortnight, he picks up a man often younger to him in order to indulge in anonymous sex. He feels such encounters would keep his life exciting. Now, students, the question is how do we categorize people like Rubin and Donald after looking into these cases? Are they homosexual, heterosexual, bisexual or just difficult to put them into any of these categories?

The class got over after some time and a student, named Sourav approached Rajendra Sir.

"Rajendra Sir, can I have a word with you", asked Sourav.

"Sure, go ahead," Professor Rajendra replied.

"My name is Sourav, I am a new student. I missed your earlier classes and would like to meet you to get an insight."

The professor replied, "Welcome to our university, Sourav! People here call me Raj. I am travelling tomorrow to attend an event. You can meet me early next week to clarify all your doubts. Now, if you will excuse me, my girlfriend (pointing to a white Premier Padmini delight) is waiting to go for a long drive," says Raj with a twinkle in his eyes.

Sourav smiled and said, "Sure sir. Thank you for your time."

Raj nodded in affirmation and moved towards the car. He opened the door and stepped in the driver's seat with a smile on his face. He is ready to go for a long drive, his natural stress buster. This is the time he always looked forward to after a long and tiring day and wanted to cherish every moment of it. Without any further delay, he turned on the keys to spend some 'me' time far from the hustle and bustle of the monotonous city life. No sooner has he taken the highway, he noticed a beautiful, young woman standing near a lamp post on the isolated road. As the cool wind brushed her hair pleasantly, Raj looked out of the driver's seat and slowed down to ask her if she would need a lift.

He asked politely, "Madam, do you need a lift?"

[Song being played]

Rote hue aate hai sab, hansataa huaa jo jaaegaa

Vo muqaddar kaa sikandar jaaneman kahalaaegaa…

(Everyone arrives crying, but the one who exits laughing

Will be called the king of destiny, my dear…)

The woman, as though coming out of her reverie, looked at Raj with a surprised expression. She managed to say, "Yes perhaps. That would be helpful. Thanks!" Then she looked around and asked, "But where do I sit? Behind you or next to you?"

Raj smiled and said, "Madam, you may sit anywhere; people would still think me as the driver!"

"In that case, I shall sit in the front," the woman looked amused.

"Madam, please close the window. Heavy wind is blowing, looks like it's going to rain", Raj said sounding very concerned.

"My name is Kusum, not madam!" she corrected.

"Oh okay. Nice! My name is Raj," he revealed.

"Raj Kapoor?", Kusum laughed and looked at him.

"Not really. Only Raj," he smiled and said.

"Hmm. I see." Kusum said. After a brief pause, Raj asked her, "Kusum, aren't you afraid to travel with an unknown person, that also a man?"

Kusum asked back promptly, "Why would I be afraid of traveling with anyone? Do you have any wrong intentions?"

"Oh God! Do I look like a villain to you?" Raj was equally quick to ask.

Kusum laughed out loud and said, "No no. I didn't mean that. You seem to be a jovial and an educated man!"

"Hmm. Am I? Glad to hear that." Raj smiled and said.

"You're! No wonder this song is getting repeated", Kusum said while rolling her eyes in admiration.

"Somehow I am in love with this song. However, you may change the tape", Raj said pointing towards the deck

"Hmm. Let's hear Lata didi's songs", Kusum said picking a tape from the deck

So, tell me Kusum, what were you doing on a highway like this? asked Raj.

"Well, Mr. Raj, what does a woman do on a highway? Either she is waiting for a client or is a client herself", said Kusum.

"What?" Raj gave a sudden break. "Are you a ...?", he asked.

"Men cannot think anything beyond sex, can they?" Kusum asked calmly, looking annoyed. "Well, for your information, I was waiting for a goddam bus for a long time but didn't get any. Shall we move now? Kusum asked.

"My apologies..." Raj said.

After a brief moment of silence, he again asked, "If you don't take it otherwise, can I say something?"

"Hmm. Go on", said Kusum.

"The color of your saree is good", Raj said hesitantly, not intending to sound flattering.

"Ha ha! Are you trying to say that I am looking good in this saree?!" Kusum asked lifting her eyebrows.

Raj smiled.

"Who wouldn't look beautiful for a wedding?", asked Kusum.

"Are you a runaway bride then?", Raj asked, looking perplexed.

"Ha ha! No I am not, but a run away marriage attendee", clarified Kusum.

Raj asked curiously, "Runaway marriage attendee, what do you mean?"

Kusum explained, "Rukmini, my friend fell in love with someone but was forcibly being married away to someone else. I did not like to be a part of such a fake wedding, so I ran away from the venue."

"Hmm. I see. I wish people value the power of love and consider it enough for two people to share a life together. But sadly, this seldom happens, isn't it?," Raj remarked.

"Well, if you ask me, I would say that love isn't enough because there is always a suspicion within us. This has led to a phenomenon called marriage! In reality, it all has to do with a man's prestige", said Kusum.

"But, I thought that it's a woman's desire to marry or not – this also counts too", said Raj.

Kusum opined, "Partially true, but largely untrue! There was a time when a man's prestige or social status was counted by how many wives he had. This was followed by how many children he produced. Soon, there will be a time when a man's prestige will be counted by how many divorce or affairs he has".

"Hmm. We are passing by my residential block; can we stop by for a quick lunch? My mother prepares awesome *Machher Jhol* (typical Bengali Fish curry) and Sandesh (sweet)." Raj said with a childlike innocence in his eyes.

"But why to trouble her? Can't we eat on the way in some good *Daba*; it would be my treat," asked Kusum

"You know, most of the days I end up eating lunch outside, but today would be one such lucky day when I get a chance to have pure homemade food. Don't feel shy, Kusum. I hope you would be fine to join me for somber lunch in my humble abode," said Raj.

Kusum was unsure but eventually gave in. Raj parked the car; they both got down and made their way to the door to ring the doorbell. They waited there for few seconds before an elderly lady opened the door for them. She was dressed in a traditional Bengali saree, wore *Sakha pola* (the typical red and white bangles that Bengali married women wear) in both her hands, and a large red bindi on her forehead. Kusum noticed her kind eyes and warm smile.

"Raju, my child, did you get married? She is beautiful, what is your name?", she continued.

"Maa, can we come in or you would ask all these questions standing in the doorway itself?" asked Raj feeling embarrassed.

Kusum folded her hands and greeted her, "Nomoskar Mashima (aunty), my name is Kusum. I was waiting on the highway for a bus and your son was kind enough to offer me a lift. That is how I am here."

"Oh!" She exclaimed. "I thought something else, anyways both of you freshen up while I tell Ramu to serve lunch."

When they were alone again, Kusum asked, "How many names do you have, Mr. Raj?"

Raj explained, "My real name is Rajendra, Maa calls me Raju (pet name) and I call myself Raj. You know, Kusum, Bengalis have two names – one, *bhalo naam* (means good name), that is for everyone to know, and two, *dak naam* (means pet name), that is only for the closed ones to know."

They made their way to the table where a very simple Bengali lunch is spread. Raju's mother said, "I have prepared very simple food, keeping Raju's hectic schedule in mind. He doesn't have any fixed time to return home."

Kusum said, "Mashima, any food that is prepared with love would satisfy the mind first and the hunger later unlike hotel food that does satisfy the hunger but the mind craves for something better. There is nothing like home cooked food."

Mashima said, "Ok dear. Sit down and have your lunch. So, Kusum, what do you do? Are you studying or working somewhere?"

"I have done my B.A. (Psychology), I mean 15th standard", Kusum said.

"Oh, I see! Our Raju (she pauses and thinks for a while) has just finished 12th standard", Raju's mom said.

"Maa please, I have studied till 19th standard, you seem to have forgotten." Raju corrected.

"No Raju, you were in 10th standard when your father fell sick, remember?" Maa said.

Kusum broke the silence, "Ha ha! Raj that's fine to have studied till 12th standard and there is nothing to feel ashamed of it. Maa has given you true-life experience than just a piece of paper." The atmosphere was light and both the mother and son burst out in laughter. Soon after, Raj and Kusum finished their food and prepared to leave. Kusum touched mashima's feet as a mark of respect before leaving the house.

Mashima said, "May God bless you. Please visit again." Kusum nodded in affirmation.

Back in the car, Raj noticed that Kusum was very calm and quiet. She looked absent minded, lost in her own thoughts. So, he asked her, "Kusum, what happened? You have become silent all of a sudden. All well?"

Kusum looked at Raj and said slowly, "Missing my mother."

"You would see her in a while, right?" Raj asked.

"I wish that was true. But, the reality is I will never be able to see her." Kusum said with her wide open eyes.

"Oh sorry! Is she with God?" Raj asked.

"No. Why do you want to kill a living person?" Kusum said

"Then, why can't you meet her?" Raj asked.

Kusum revealed slowly, "My full name is S. Kusum Chatterjee born to a Bengali mother. My father is non-Bengali though. My birth did bring happiness to my parents and grandparents proclaiming to others that they are also capable of producing children and proving an ability to multiply in number. I learnt from my grandmother that Sandesh was distributed in the entire colony when I was born. People were often perplexed about my gender – some said that since the child is soft, she must be a girl while others felt that I am a boy. As I grew up, I realized that it's so difficult to interact with a person without knowing the gender. May be we are programmed like that! A program that runs to mention the social aspects of one's biological sex and behaviors associated with it. In the name of 'culture,' I was taught the do's and don't's of gender traits and …(pauses).

"Hmm. Why are you so much interested in gender roles?" Raj asked looking confused.

"Because it has do with my past, present and future. My entire identity. Because I don't fit into the conventional male female category. I don't belong anywhere" Kusum was firm yet polite and looked away as she said this. Raj noticed that her eyes looked sad and she swallowed her tears. He assured her by saying, "I am listening, if you want to tell me."

Kusum looked into his eyes and said, "I don't know why, but I feel like trusting you! Strangers often don't meet in life. I have a feeling its fine to tell you."

"That's correct. You can certainly trust a stranger sometimes", Raj said.

Kusum started narrating the story of her life. "My real name isn't Kusum. 'S' has to do with something with my full name! My father was an aggressive doctor while my mother was soft and kind. She was the one who took care of the entire household. My father always tried to exhibit his masculine traits by remaining emotionally undemonstrative and expected my mother to show some feminine traits. His firm patriarchal self always expected my mother to 'follow' his orders. My mom always obliged so as to maintain peace at home. All these years I have seen several people idolize their role models who depicts masculinity and femininity. As I recall, I was five year old these traits were put into my head to differentiate sexes. I couldn't understand what was happening to me as I was expected to showcase the so called 'masculine' traits but deep down, I was drawn towards the 'feminine' traits. I was forced to play with cars (toys), thinking of becoming a doctor or pilot and be sought after by opposite gender as opposed to playing with dolls, or watching some movies or appreciating the same sex. All these was considered sacrilegious. Often, my father rebuked me by saying, 'God made his mistake by making you a boy.' He would punish me for any activity that had femininity attached to it or doing any 'girly stuff'. While I was punished, I was not supposed to cry and was forced to shut all my emotions. This often got replaced with feelings of anger towards him and impending grudges against him.

We were forced to accompany father to his several conferences. We were presented as his token of victory and a mark of his fake and empty pride. My mother had this constant pressure to 'maintain' her figure and in order to appear beautiful to showcase others of his ability to maintain a luxurious life. We were mere puppets to his make-believe world. As a child, I discovered quite early in life that society thrives on superficiality. Look at the magazine covers, television advertisements or movies that emphasis only on outward appearance. One of my friends, Sharmila wanted to become an actor but she was rejected every time she went for an audition on the pretext that she had a typical plain Jane appearance and not the kick-ass one that was required for the role. Though my mother didn't like these conferences or meetings but she chose to obey my father's demands every time. I understood this while pursuing psychology that the male gender is looked during marriage proposal as a provider and thus he ought to be aggressive. My mother had resigned herself to fate, chose not to be independent anymore and had accepted this stereotyping. Her ignorance often reflected to me that gender role is often more complicated than just the categorically splitting into the male and female frame.

Every time, we were to go to a conference together, he would brief us on how to greet people, how to talk, sit and how much to talk etc. These sessions were painfully boring and to my young mind, they only showed his negative characteristics. I hated him to the core. Sometimes, this checklist was often narrated while getting into car as well. He also lectured on the type of gifts I should accept in such gatherings. I was supposed to deny the gifts that was meant for girls, as they were sometimes mistakenly given out thinking that children would accept anything. I had to reject mentioning that, it's for girls! This made him very happy and triumphant. In reality, I missed those jelly chocolates, strawberry filled sweets and others. I had to eat dark chocolates that never satisfied my taste buds. My father's eyes were constantly on me and they followed me everywhere. I was instructed to look out for his affirmation or non-affirmation sign before accepting or rejecting any gifts.

In one such conference, our family got introduced to Dr. Banerjee's family who were supposed to move into our neighboring building. Dr. Banerjee had a son, named Debu who was six year older to me. After I met him, I had this some kind of unknown attraction towards him. As luck would have it, he also joined the same school as mine when they moved in to the neighboring building within a week of the conference.

Often, while I got into my school bus, some of the older boys often bullied me by calling out 'girl' or 'sissy' because of my feminine look and the girls would giggle on hearing these comments. Earlier no one sat next to me, but Debu, brought the much needed change to it. He would sit next to me and hold my hand in such a way that wouldn't let anyone know. I sat looking outside from my window seat and he kept looking on the other side without even uttering a word. He saved me from several such calamities. Unlike the past, I hated to go to school but now, with Debu around, I looked forward to go to school. His small but caring gestures made me happy and won my heart.

On Sundays, I would visit his home to play. My father didn't restrict me as Debu looked manly by appearance and so he was safe in my father's eyes. But, a thing that often disheartened me was, Dr. Banerjee would call me as younger brother of Debu. However, Debu never called me his brother! I still smile at times remembering those days.

My feelings for Debu was growing stronger with each passing day. One day, while we were playing, I accumulated the courage to kiss him on his cheek. My heart was thumping and a shiver ran down in my spine as I walked towards him. He stood like to wax doll till our kiss lasted. We looked into each other's eye and were oblivious of our surroundings.

Kusum paused as though reminiscing those moments that were so deeply etched in her heart. Then suddenly, coming out from her reverie, she pointed to the rainbow on a nearby mountain and said to Raj in a child like innocence.

"Hey Raj, look out here! Such a beautiful rainbow has adorned the sky." She then started humming some lines from a poetry.

Little, little drop of dew
Little, little dew of hope
Little, little hope of formation
Little, little formation of life
Little, little made a meaning to live and love

Raj looked at her with surprise in his eyes. "You hymn and sing very well. Where did you learn this poetry from?"

Kusum blushed and said, "I read this poem in a book written by Dr. Mukherjee, a famous psychologist. I am big fan of him, you see." She started chirping it again.

Raj said, "I see. You were telling me something about Debu!"

"Ahh yes, Debu, my love! As we looked into each other's eye and kissed his strawberry lips, we didn't realize that we had a witness, who was none other than Dr. Banerjee himself. He was standing aghast at the door and all hell broke loose. He obviously couldn't accept the fact that his son was more than a brother to me!" Kusum said with a tinge of wit.

"Oh, then what happened?", Raj asked.

"The inevitable happened of course. In less than a week's time, Dr. Banerjee's family shifted to some other town without telling anyone about the incident. He didn't wanted his home to be the hub of such shameful activities that would only bring disgrace. Debu came to meet me in the wee hours to bid adieu. He kissed me on my forehead before leaving," Kusum said with a smile.

She continued, "Yet at times, learned people show ignorance as well. There are two reasons to state, firstly, they know the theory and its applications but they often mistakably believe its applicable on others but not on oneself. In spite of knowing that its socially constructed taboo, even the learned becomes blind. As children grow in the society age grading happens automatically, that makes one aware of social positions and related behaviors are expected. In a psychology book on *Childhood Sexuality* it describes how children at early age might engage in sexual behavior to understand gender roles to receive a sense of being cared for, though it might not be motivated for sexual desires. Secondly, Dr. Banjeree did what any parents would do for the betterment of their children."

Raj said, "It must have been the most heart-wrecking moment for you after Debu moved away."

Kusum replied, "Frankly, a vacuum was created that gradually became intolerable and that became heart wrecking."

"What do you mean by that?," Raj asked.

"I lived with those moments spent with Debu for the next few years. Debu's large penetrating eyes and his kiss became my fantasy till I turned 16. When the house was empty on some occassions, I would take out my mom's *Tant saree* from her wardrobe, drape myself in it and would stand in front of the mirror for long hours admiring myself. I would wonder if Debu would love to see me like this." Kusum revealed.

"Hmm. What happened after you turned 16?,"Raj was curious to know.

Kusum continued, "Dr. Mukherjee's observation in his book *Love for the Lonely*, 'Real truth and real love go together' was apt in my situation. My mother had accepted the truth about my preference but my father seemed to live in a world of seclusion and non-acceptance. I had to play a dual role, that is, project the so called male traits at conferences or parties and the real traits in isolation. I was forced to ask a girl out in the party for a dance or a drink as a mark of masculine behavior but in reality I was yearning to be with Debu. All that mattered to my father, was conferences, parties and social interactions. In one of the state level conferences of surgeons, our family bumped into Dr. Banerjee's family. Although it was an awkward moment for Dr. Banerjee recalling the incident but he hesitantly wished our family and made his way to grab a drink. My father perhaps had understood the reasons behind Dr. Banerjee's family shifting to another town. My eyes were looking for Debu as soon as Dr. Banerjee made a way for himself.

I learnt that day Dr. Banerjee kept his family in seclusion with a fear that his son Debu and I might often meet in such gathering. After a while, Debu walked into the conference with a good-looking girl. His father was introducing his son to others, as someone who had graduated in medicine and was now set to pursue Masters in Surgery. Many families were eager to meet this young doctor, who was standing tall wearing a warm smile on his face and looked handsome in an attractive brown suit. He could be a prospective groom in the marriage market. I noticed that his lips were still like strawberry.

There was an air of superficiality though, when Dr. Banerjee hesitantly introduced him to us pointing out his son's achievements in medicine and capabilities of becoming a great follower of his father footsteps. This was an introduction that was aimed to pass a message to us that his Debu likes women, I thought. Who was he trying to convince, anyway? But, matters of the heart is different, you see; and my thumping heart told me that Debu still feels towards me those emotions called love. As we kept dancing changing our partners, I had several eye contacts with him."

Kusum suddenly stopped to ask Raj about the weather outside. Raj replied, You mean monsoon, right? Yes, to a certain extent! Were you happy to meet Debu again? Raj asked trying to bring her back to the topic.

Kusum replied, The answer is both yes and no! If you've read Dr. Mukherjee's book *Love and Kindness*, you will agree to me, I suppose. I liked where he mentions that the challenge with people admitting while being in love is, 'A real change in heart can bring true peace and joy.' This can happen when the heart pours out what it contains within it. He also proves with several case studies that this act of kindness is missing in love. One fine day, while I was walking towards my college, a person stopped his scooter to ask if I needed lift like the way you asked me today. That person was Debu. I was obviously surprised to see him. I sat behind him without uttering a word till we reached a discreet place. As soon as we got down from the scooter, he hugged me and gave the same tender kiss on my forehead. We talked long enough and stood there to witness the beautiful sun set. He asked me that what I would have done if we never met? I just sang Rabindrath Tagore's song to answer his question.

Jodi tor dak sune keu na ashe,
Tobe ekla cholo,
Ekla chalo,
Ekla chalo re,
Ekla cholo re

[If no one answers your call,
Then walk along,
(be no afraid) walk alone my friend.]

For the next two years, we kept meeting each other only to pretend in all social gatherings that nothing is cooking between us. This helped us to maintain our sanity. But, as luck would have it, my conscience started questioning me often and I felt that we both were cheating ourselves by trying hard to play the dual roles. How long would this continue? Debu understood my feelings patiently and disclosed that he pursued specialization in surgery to help people like me. He wanted me to undergo a *sex change* operation so that we could marry safely. I was in for anything that would make us live together.

I decided to break the news to my family and as I expected, it had its ripple effect - my father out rightly rejected my decision and threatened me with dire consequences – denying me of my share of property and the family name. I was asked to leave. My mother was a mere puppet in his hand, and so she was forced to stay quiet on this matter. However, she gave me her gold and some money secretly in due course of time. With these, I stepped out of my house forever.

Debu took care of my basic needs. After some days, we decided that I should not delay the surgery any further; so I went under the knife in various stages. Gradually, I could see my dreams turning into reality. Debu would often stay with me during the evenings and we would chat for long hours in the wide balcony overlooking the lake nearby. The cool breeze would soothe us and we would be lost in each other's embrace. I was starting to feel that everything will be fine and the bits and pieces of my life would finally fall in place. Little did I know that destiny had some other plans and that darkness was lurking behind to cast an inevitable spell in my life that was to last forever. My villainous father was furious to know about the support I received from my mother and Debu. He felt that my existence on the earth is wrong and it's against the forces of nature. He couldn't accept that his child was not what he desired. So, he decided to kill my happiness forever. He called up Dr. Banerjee to inform about my decision and to warn him to save his son from the clutches of his devil possessed son. Dr. Banerjee couldn't think in his wildest dream that Debu is still seeing me and that the situations are now out of control. So, he decided to take action in a cunning way. He stalked Debu for next few days to know the truth. He knew that if he had confronted his son or caught him red-handed, he might have walked away from his house and property. He couldn't have stopped his son legally as well. So, he played it safe!

Kusum paused and asked Raj, "Raj, why don't we stop for a cup of coffee?"

(Kusum bought two cups of coffee. While sipping their coffee, they both were lost in their own thoughts)

"Don't you want to know, what happened next?" Kusum asked breaking the silence. Raj nods his head to indicate yes.

"One evening, Dr. Banerjee mentioned to Debu about a proposal from a well-known doctor from the west. The girl was an anesthetist and her family is well known in that region. Dr. Banerjee made Debu to realize that having an anesthetist in the family will be beneficial and the collaborative work of a surgeon and an anesthetist would take the hospital to higher level (growth). He stressed on the challenges that they often face in the hospital due to lack of good anesthetists. He also mentioned that he is aware of his son's secret love affair. He made Debu to realize that even if he accepts me, the community would never accept and forgive. Society will ostracize them. All these will take a toll on his promising career, the future of the hospital and their standard of life – just for that one person who has undergone a sex change operation. The family would never be able to see their heir and all the efforts done in the past by Banerjee's family would become meaningless very soon. He said, "Son, our prestige is in your hands now and I assume you wouldn't hurt the family expectations."

Kusum continued, "Debu came to see me the next day as usual in the evening. I was busy preparing his favorite fish fry in the kitchen. He was standing with a lost expression on his face while looking outside the window. He slowly told me about the conversations that took place between the father-son duo. When I asked him about his decision, he mentioned that his father would shoot himself in case he marries me and spoils the family name. He added that he is confused but in Debu's confusion, I got my answer -

Jodi sobai thake muhk phirae ,
sobai kore bhoye,
Tobe poran khule, O tui, mukh phute tor moner kotha,
Ekla bolo re … Ekla cholo re

(If no one talks to you, O my unlucky friend,
If no one speaks to you,
If everyone looks the other way and everyone is afraid, Then bare your soul and let out what is in your mind, (be not afraid)
Speak alone my friend … (be not afraid) walk alone my friend.)

Debu hugged me one last time as I continued to hum these lines while tears rolled down my eyes. He said 'sorry' as he stepped out of my house…"

"Kusum, the tissue paper box is on the upper deck", Raj said.

"Thanks Raj", Kusum uttered while wiping her tears with the tissues.

"Sorry to hear that you had a heartbreaking moment.", Raj said after a pause unsure of what to say next. Words fall short when feelings take over.

Kusum went on, "It wasn't just heartbreaking but it broke my identity! All that anguish that was deep hidden in me because rejections from family and friends started to pour out like a current in the sea that would seem destructive. Several questions that kept swelling out of silent scream, why did this happen to me? Why God didn't have mercy on me? If I had been 'male' or 'female', life would have been different. But, 'she-male'? Society is always harsh on people like us. As I was muddled in these questions and was seeking an answer, a song that always kept me alive was getting played on radio. It goes something like this..."

Jab kali ghata chaye,
Ore o re o andhera sach ko nigal jaye
Jab duniya sari, dar ke age sar apna jhukaye,

Tu shola banja, Wo shola banja, Jo khud jal ke jahan raushan karde,
Ekla jalo re.

(When dark clouds cover the sky, When darkness engulfs the truth,
When the world cowers and bows before fear,
You be the flame, The flame that burns you and banishes darkness from the world,
(be not afraid) Burn alone my friend.)

Seeking an answer to bring down the burning turmoil within me became mandatory in order to exist. I wanted to rise like the phoenix bird from my own ashes; I was determined to say hello to life. I would sit in a park to seek answers in isolation. Some days I would sit in a temple to seek answers from the Almighty. As I walked back home through a tunnel after being at the park or the temple, the tunnel at times became my hope metaphorically. A train passes through the darkness to see light at the end of tunnel. The days went by quite fast but the nights were painfully long. Depression started engulfing me gradually and it took a toll on my life.

"I finally found solace while being seated near a pond that was surrounded by mountains. This beautiful place was just a few blocks away from my home. The best time one would pass time is by occasionally throwing pebbles to see it making a noise as it dives down forever by creating a ripple. After few silent observations, I kept throwing different sized pebbles, the larger one, created more the impact by forming larger ripples. If the same pebble was thrown at an angle slightly horizontal it would touch superficial layer of water that would touch water hittting across few layers of ripples to dive far across the earlier version of throwing pebbles. Some pebbles made their way to the shore. This repetitive task gave me answers to all my questions. These questions were raised because I am like a pebble that fell deep into the society (water) that would know to sallow through making noise and creating disturbance (ripples) on ones choice. But I forgot in fostering trust with loved ones that destiny is in my own head like the same pebble that did get touched by water, passed through the hurdles of ripples without sinking easily to make a way through a shore." Kusum went on as her eyes welled up in tears.

Raj offered the tissue paper box as he slowed down the car.

"Raj, cha khabe? (Would you like some tea?)," Kusum asked suddenly. Raj nodded in affirmation and goes on to pick the 'bhar' (an earthen teacup) to sip tea.

"Raj, what happened? You seem to be curious to ask some questions", Kusum said.

"How do you know that?," Raj asked

"Your reflexing muscles are hinting so", Kusum said managing a smile on her face.

"I hope you won't feel bad if some questions are asked just out of curiosity. Please remember it's just out of a concern rather than anything else", Raj reassured. Kusum lifts her right hand to indicate to ask as she sips tea.

"Debu knew everything about you, then why did he put his foot down at the last moment?"Raj asked

Kusum replied, "As far as I think, there are several reasons to it: firstly, Debu's father and my father played villains in our lives. This apart, since Debu's practice was getting recognized and he was very close to taste success, his proximity with me would have spoiled his success and hampered his meteoric rise. Debu's father was successful in injecting this thing in his head. Additionally, his family knew that I couldn't conceive and have my own children. One of the objectives of Indian marriage is to satisfy the parents by making them grandparents as soon as possible. This was impossible in our case, until adoption was accepted. Finally, Debu had choices to make, you know." Kusum pointed out calmly.

"Hmm. Sad to know this! I have another thing to ask, just out of curiosity again! Did you happen to meet Debu again?" Raj asked.

"My love towards Debu had purity. We never crossed the line, till things fell in place by itself. It was he who had turned down, denied and walked away from the relationship. As I am a woman now, I didn't want to provoke the dignity of women. Hence I didn't feel like going behind him." Kusum said with conviction.

"Nice! I respect your opinion. Does it mean that, you aren't in love with him?" Raj asked with his curious eyes.

"As I mentioned that he walked away, for some time (months) I terribly missed him. It was a like 'Phantom limb', it is like there is a sensation of missing limb that would seem to be attached to the body and is moving appropriately with other body parts while my daily routine continued in his absence. I think we all have such 'limb' till the acceptance stage", Kusum said.

"Yes I have nothing much less to agree with you". Raj said

"Raj, it's getting dark, let's leave now," Kusum suggested

"Are you afraid of darkness?," Raj asked curiously

"Earlier I was, now no more", said Kusum adjusting her seat belt.

"What do you mean by that?" Raj asked.

"After accepting the bitter truth of society, I set myself out to lead a life for myself entirely. I realized that the poisonous tentacles of society does not spare anyone, especially people like us. Once I realized, I became strong from within.

One day, I stumbled upon an ad displayed in the town library for an assistance librarian position that has just opened up. Being a voracious reader (a habit that I inherited from my mom) myself, I decided to apply. I already knew Maria, the librarian there. She was sweet and liberal in her thoughts. She had understood me, on learning the kind of books that I picked to read. Maria assured to get my application accepted and recommended by name to the board. Though there were some initial hitches, but her assurance helped me to get a job." Kusum said all these with a broad smile on her face. For the first time, Raj noticed that her smile was beautiful.

"That was a very nice gesture by Maria", Raj acknowledged.

"Definitely, it was my first real acceptance and I am both proud and grateful for that...Raj, slow down the car", Kusum shouted out of anxiety. In a fit of fear, she clutched his hand tightly.

"Sorry, I was looking at you and missed to see the herd of sheep.", Raj as he applied the sudden break.

"I'm sorry", Kusum said loosening her hand from Raj's hand

"I didn't mind", said Raj by taking off his eye from her to start his car

"Kusum, you were mentioning real acceptance," Raj wanted to know.

"Yes! For the first time I met a person, who showcased unconditional love. Maria had empathy with my situation. After the library closed for the day, she would sit with me to read books. At several times, she dozed off to sleep in her seat trying to read a book. I had understood that she wanted me to support and encourage me to fulfill my dreams. One evening I was stacking the books into the respective sections, Maria interrupted me to talk something. She asked me, if I am keen to study further. I immediately jumped upon to say 'yes'. Among several books I read, Dr.Mukherjee's book which influenced and motivated me to pursue psychology. His writings reflected several truths of people like me."

Maria spoke to a community college principal about me and made a request to offer a seat to pursue studies. Although he was reluctant, Maria's assertive skills mellow down the aggressive behavior of college management. I was asked to visit the college next day to submit the application. As I walked into the college, people could hardly make out I'm she-male. I was set to fill out the admission form; there wasn't any section apart from male and female to tick an option from gender question. I choose female! I choose to be open to people from that day onwards. Maria had told me, 'Make people and situation powerless by not reacting to reactions from the society' before I set out to begin a new journey to create a new identity. She was right as it had humility! Today I feel proud to say, I am She-male, Kusum said triumphantly.

"It's truly an inspirational gratitude from Maria to help you to create your own identity," marked Raj.

"Yes! I became powerful by making others powerless otherwise Kusum wouldn't have existed. Otherwise several other Kusum's wouldn't have dared to open up to others", Kusum said.

"Hmm. By the way, you didn't tell me your real name", Raj looked at her in anticipation.

"Well, my real name will get buried with me in my grave", said Kusum winking her eyes.

"You being a nice person, I am sure you would find someone very soon", Raj said in hesitation after coughing in order to adjust his throat.

"Raj, could you stop near that lamp-post? I shall get down there", Kusum said.

"I shall drop you at your doorstep", Raj said slowing down the car

"That's perfectly fine! I appreciate your help, but I would prefer to walk till my home", Kusum said.

"What's the matter?" Raj asked.

"Raj, I understand your feelings. See this, Dr. Mukherjee's, latest release (book) and he says, 'It's complete normal for a person to get attracted towards the opposite sex, especially for a man towards woman on hearing an emotional story.' Even I liked your patience of hearing my story, and empathy that helped me to feel better. However, I don't want to have another Debu in my life. I know its wrong to compare but I am not sure if I can handle another heartbreak", Kusum said as she opened the car door to step out.

"I really started to like you, Kusum. Are you sure on your decision?" Raj asked.

"I shall promise one thing, if we meet again on a highway like today I shall see if the 'like' can convert to 'love' ", Kusum said in an assuring tone while closing the car door.

Before leaving, Kusum bend down outside the car window and asked, "By the way Raj, what is your full name?"

Raj replied calmly with a smile on his face, "Kusum, I am in your hand. My full name is Dr. Rajendra Mukherjee."

Kusum stands perplexed hearing that he is her admirer. She extends her book to take autograph.

"You are what you choose to be"

We would like to thank the following reviewers

(Alphabetic orders of their name)
If someone's name is missed, it's accidentally not intentionally

Abhilash Alwandi

Sr Agatha

Aishwarya Deengar

Akhil Teja

Akanksha

Anjali

Bhakti M

Biswanth

Chittajit Mitra

Deepak Sharma

Deepika Bhardwaj

Dhivya Balaji

Jalem Raj Rohit

Jayashree

Jishnu Bhattachary

Jyothi Babel

Jyothi Byhatti

Kalyan Panja

Lenin

Madhusmita P

Maniaparna   Sengupta

Majumder

Merril Anil

Mutturaj Hulagabal

Mounika Lakkakula

N K Narasimhan

Nandhini

Natasha Borah Khan

Nandhini

Chandrasekran

Nikhil

Nikita

Nishtha Singh

Nithish Jayasheela

Pankaj Goyal

Parul Thakur

Pradeep T

Primrosetina

Phani Raj

Rachna Gupta

Rajashree Ghosh

Romila

Ruchita Shah

Sachin Kodagali

Sahil Narain

Santosh Panda

Satya Subramanyam

Sheetal

Shilpa Patil

Shwetha H S

Solomon Manoj

Sujeeth Kumar

Swathi Shenoy

Tahseen

Sr Victoria

Vikalp Trivedi

Vince George

Santosh Avvannavar: Santosh started his career as a consultant and Soft Skills Trainer. After his college education from NITK, Surathkal, he worked as a researcher at University of Eindhoven, University of Twente, and Indian Institute of Science, Bangalore. He was also the Placement President while working at IISC, Bangalore. He has over twenty-five publications of mostly research documents in national and international journals. He has also authored sixteen conference papers and regularly writes articles for a national and worldwide daily paper. He also works as an advisor for different organizations.

He also dabbles in fiction writing and is the author of *Adhuri Prem Kahaniya*; *Dear Wife, Your Husband is not a Superhero, Second Heart and Get a Job WITHOUT an Interview; Be A B.A.; Surrogate Author; Title is Untitled; Black, Grey and White; The Departing Point; God's Table* and *Umbilical Cord*

He likes to devote his personal time in writing for a website, namely the Amrita Foundation for HRD (www.amritafoundation.wordpress.com). He has conducted seminars and training sessions for more than 45,000 people in India and abroad over the last seven years.

Dr. Shayan Haq: Shayan is a medical doctor and cosmetologist by profession working at Bijapur, Karnataka. He is born at Gaya, Bihar and spent his quality time at West Bengal and Bihar before he moved for higher education. In his free time he loves to drive, read, watch and discuss on movies, and a gadget freak.

Editor
Profile

Rajashree Ghosh: Rajashree started her career 8 years ago and went on to dabble in content writing, editing, and technical writing until motherhood happened! This wonderful phase of life made her full time mom and a part time freelancer – so far the best decision of her life. In this new phase of her life, she got an opportunity to work on myriad exciting projects. She is a post-graduate in English Literature and a self-confessed aficionado of cinema. She houses the musings of her soul in her blog https://rajashreeghosh.wordpress.com/. Married to the love of her life, she currently lives in Bangalore. She can be contacted at ghosh.rajashree@gmail.com